Fairy Tales Sticker Activity Book

priddy books

big ideas for little people

The Ugly Duckling

There was a little duckling who was not like his duckling brothers and sisters. He did not have yellow feathers like them, but was big and grey. Everyone teased the ugly duckling and made him feel sad. His mummy tried to comfort him, but was surprised at how different he was.

The ugly duckling was so sad that one day he ran away. He wandered along the river looking for other ducklings that looked like him.

Whenever he met other birds he asked them, "Have you seen any ducklings like me?" "What an ugly duckling!" they replied, "We have never seen ducklings like you before."

All winter, the duckling looked for other ducks that looked like him, but he did not find any. He was very cold and ever so lonely.

By the time spring came, the ugly duckling had grown a lot. His feathers were not grey anymore, but snow white! Then, one day, he saw some birds that looked just like him. They were flying through the sky. "Stop, stop!" he cried. "Who are you?" "We are swans, just like you", they called back. "Come with us!"

The ugly duckling was so happy as he took flight and followed them. He was not an ugly duckling after all, but had grown into a beautiful swan, with a lovely long neck and big, powerful wings.

Match and quack

Find the stickers, then draw lines to match the birds.

duck

duckling

swan

cygnet

swan

duck

cygnet

duckling

Ugly Duckling's pond

Colour in this picture of the pond.

Crown jewels

Find the jewel stickers and decorate the crown.

The Emperor's New Clothes

Can you make the Emperor's new outfit very colourful?

The Frog Prince

Can you lead the princess to the Frog Prince?

Count the frogs

Circle the frogs that are wearing a crown.

Can you count how many you have circled?

The Little Mermaid

Can you find the sea creature stickers?

How many legs does an octopus have?

Now colour in the palm tree!

Hansel and Gretel

There was once a woodcutter who had two children, Hansel and Gretel. Their nasty stepmother did not like them very much, and one day she sent them into the dark and scary forest.

Hansel left a trail of bread for them to follow back home, but the birds in the forest ate it all. "How will we get home now?" he cried.

Hansel and Gretel walked in circles until they were very tired and hungry. Finally they came across a beautiful house made entirely of gingerbread and decorated with all kinds of sweets.

The children were so hungry that they pulled off big chunks of the house and started eating. It was the most delicious thing they had ever tasted!

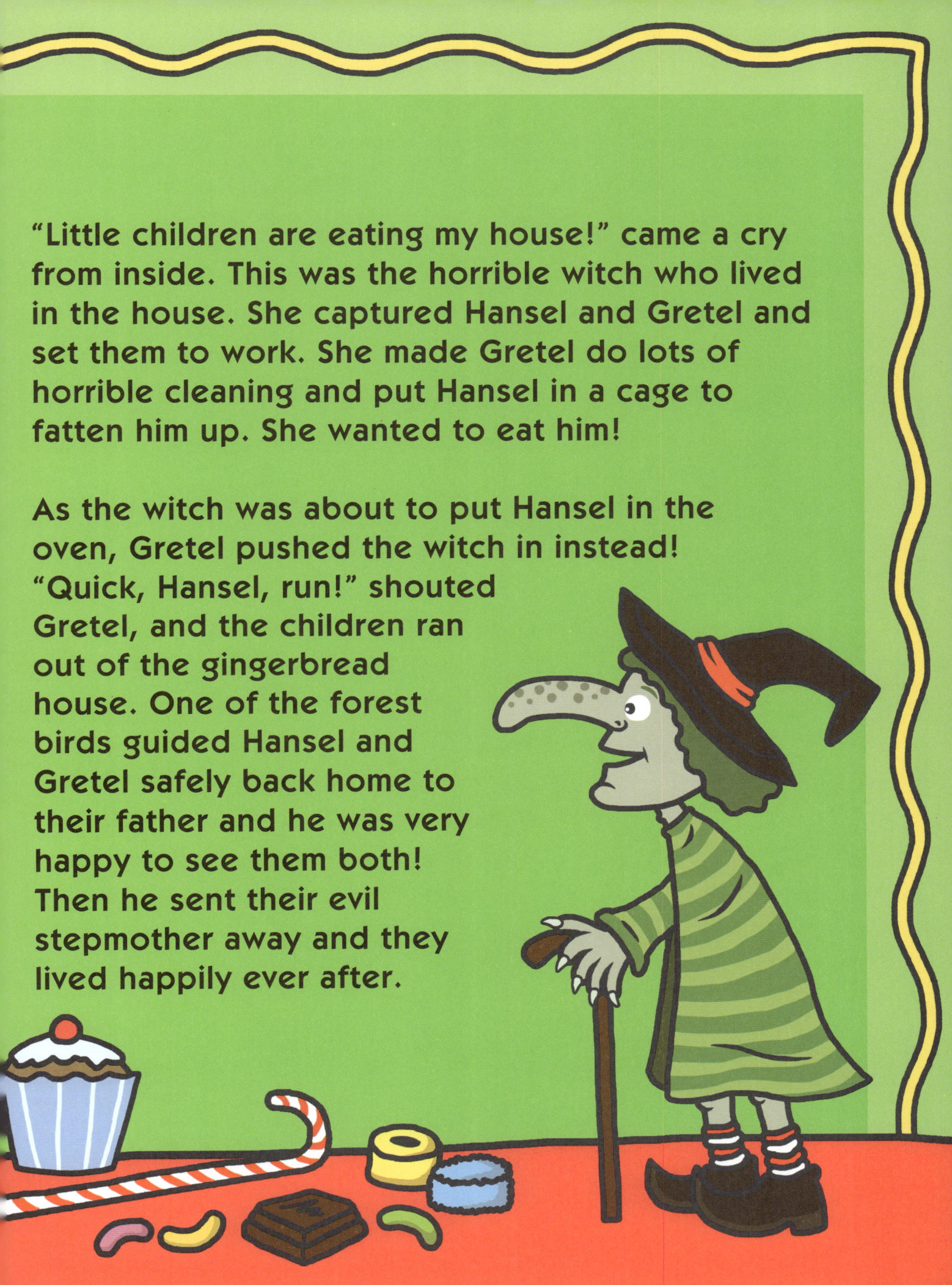

"Little children are eating my house!" came a cry from inside. This was the horrible witch who lived in the house. She captured Hansel and Gretel and set them to work. She made Gretel do lots of horrible cleaning and put Hansel in a cage to fatten him up. She wanted to eat him!

As the witch was about to put Hansel in the oven, Gretel pushed the witch in instead! "Quick, Hansel, run!" shouted Gretel, and the children ran out of the gingerbread house. One of the forest birds guided Hansel and Gretel safely back home to their father and he was very happy to see them both! Then he sent their evil stepmother away and they lived happily ever after.

Find the sweets

Decorate the roof of the house with sweetie stickers.

Hansel's trail

Find the stickers of birds to eat up Hansel's breadcrumb trail.

What colour is Gretel's skirt?

The gingerbread house

Can you find five differences between the pictures below?

Snow White's seven dwarves

Can you find seven dwarf stickers to put on the hill?

Can you find eight green apple stickers?

Sleeping Beauty

Once upon a time, there lived a king and queen who had a beautiful baby girl. They invited all the good fairies in the kingdom to a party to celebrate.

The fairies granted wishes of beauty, happiness and more for the princess. But then a bad fairy arrived and she put a curse on the royal baby: "When you are seventeen you will prick your finger on a spindle and die!" Luckily, there was one good fairy who had not yet granted her wish. She said, "The princess will not die, but will sleep until a handsome prince wakes her with a kiss!"

To stop the curse, the king banished all spindles from the kingdom. But years later, the princess found a little old lady with a spinning wheel in the castle tower. The princess had never seen a spinning wheel before so she was very curious. She pricked her finger on the spindle and, just like the kind fairy had said, she fell into a deep sleep. And the whole kingdom fell fast asleep like the princess too!

Years went by and the castle became overgrown with thorns. After 100 years, a handsome prince came from another kingdom. He cut through the thorns, climbed the castle tower and found the sleeping beauty. He kissed her and made her wake up! Soon, the whole kingdom was awake again and everyone was so happy!
The prince and princess were married and they celebrated with a big feast.

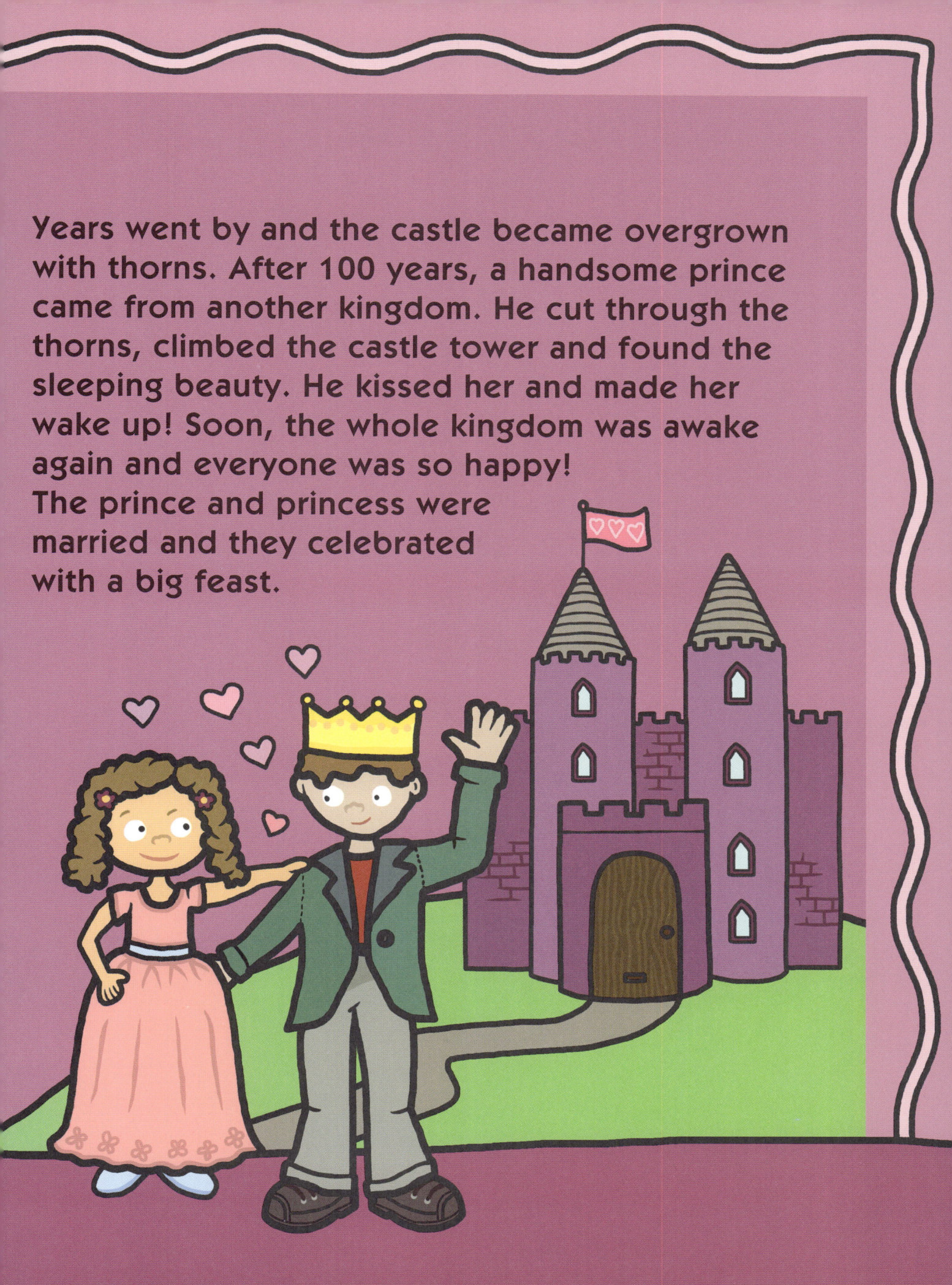

Sleeping Beauty's castle

Colour in the castle hidden in the forest.

Princess hat

Join the dots, then colour it in and add some heart stickers.

Flying fairy

Trace over the dotted line to draw the fairy.

Now colour her in.

Prince Charming

Find the stickers to complete the Prince's outfit.

Rapunzel's pretty bows

Add the pretty bows to decorate Rapunzel's long hair.

What's missing?

The three hats and the wolf's tail are missing. Find the stickers.

Little Red Riding Hood

One day, Little Red Riding Hood went to visit her grandmother on the other side of the dark wood. Before she left her mother said, "Walk quickly and don't talk to strangers!"

Little Red Riding Hood set off through the wood. Soon she came across Mr Wolf who asked her where she was going. "I'm going to see my grandmother", she said. Remembering what her mother told her, she quickly ran off.

Little Red Riding Hood stopped to pick some pretty flowers for her grandmother so it was quite late by the time she arrived at the house.

While Little Red Riding Hood had been picking flowers, mean Mr Wolf ran to grandmother's house and gobbled her up! Then, he dressed up in her nightdress and sat in her bed.

Little Red Riding Hood thought her grandmother looked a bit different, so she said, "Grandmother! What big eyes you have." "All the better to see you with!" whispered Mr Wolf.

"And what big ears you have", said Little Red Riding Hood. "All the better to hear you with!" Mr Wolf replied.

"But what big teeth you have", said Little Red Riding Hood. "All the better to eat you with!" cried Mr Wolf and jumped out of the bed!

Luckily, a friendly woodcutter came to the rescue. He made Mr Wolf spit out grandmother, and Little Red Riding Hood promised to always walk quickly and never speak to strangers again.

In the dark wood

Add some stickers to fill the wood with creatures.

Can you find Mr Wolf?

Can you
also find
a spider and
a brown
deer?

Picnic in the wood

Can you find the stickers to make a tasty picnic?

Scary Mr Wolf!

Add some more teeth stickers to Mr Wolf!

Cinderella

Add some flower stickers to Cinderella's pretty dress.

Find the glass slipper

Can you circle Cinderella's lost glass slipper?

Circle the pair of green wellington boots.

The Three Little Pigs

There were three little pigs who built three little houses. The first pig built his house out of straw. The second pig built his house out of sticks. The third pig, wanting to be really, really safe, built his house out of bricks. The little pigs loved living in their new houses.

One day, a big bad wolf came to town. First, he called at the straw house. "Let me in, let me in!" he cried. "No! Not by the hair of my chinny chin chin!" the little pig shouted back.

The wolf was angry: "I'll huff and I'll puff, and I'll blow your house down!" So he huffed and he puffed and he blew the straw house down.

The little pig ran to the stick house. Soon, the wolf knocked on the door. "Let me in, let me in!" he shouted. "No! Not by the hair of our chinny chin chins!" The little pigs cried.

The wolf was very angry: "I'll huff and I'll puff, and I'll blow your house down!" So he huffed and he puffed and he blew the stick house down.

The two little pigs ran to the brick house, but the wolf followed them and said, "Let me in, let me in!" "No! Not by the hair of our chinny chin chins!" the little pigs shouted back. "I'll huff and I'll puff, and I'll blow your house down!" said the wolf again. So he huffed and he puffed but he couldn't blow the brick house down.

The wolf climbed onto the roof and down the chimney. He landed with a splash in a big pot of boiling water. The wolf was in a stew and the little pigs were saved!

The straw house

Can you spot five differences between the pictures below?

Three Little Pigs maze

Can you find a route to the brick house avoiding the wolf?

Goodnight pigs

Find the stickers to complete the scene.

Wishing star

How colourful can you make the big star?

Magic wand

Join the dots to finish the magical wand.

Jack and the Beanstalk

Once upon a time, there was a little boy called Jack. One day, Jack's mother sent him to market to sell their cow because they did not have any food. On the way he met a man who offered to swap the cow for some magic beans.

Jack's mother was very angry that he had swapped the cow for some beans, so she threw them out of the window!

The next day, Jack woke up to find a huge beanstalk had grown in the garden! He climbed and climbed up the beanstalk. At the top there was a magical castle where a mean giant lived. Outside the castle Jack met a fairy. She told Jack the giant had captured a goose that could lay golden eggs. "You must rescue the goose and all your problems will be solved", she told Jack.

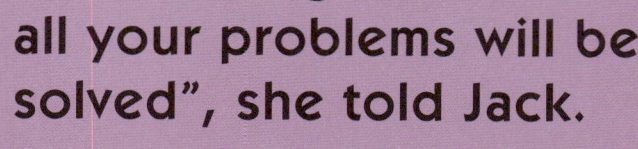

Jack sneaked into the house and hid in a cupboard while the giant was eating.

On the table he saw the beautiful goose in a cage! When the giant had fallen asleep, Jack grabbed the cage.

The giant woke up! "Fee-fi-fo-fum! I smell the blood of an Englishman!" He chased Jack out of the castle and down the beanstalk, all the while shouting, "Fee-fi-fo-fum! I smell the blood of an Englishman!"

When he got to the bottom of the beanstalk, Jack ran for an axe and chopped the stalk down before the giant could climb down too.

Now that they had the goose that could lay golden eggs, Jack and his mother never had to worry about going hungry again.

Help Jack match

Draw lines between the pairs of matching characters.

Climb the beanstalk

Can you add some green leaf stickers to the beanstalk?

Now count how many leaves you have added.

Billy Goat's Gruff

Can you find some stickers to decorate the scene?

Can you find an orange fish and purple butterfly sticker too?

Tom Thumb

Find the sticker of Tom Thumb and put him in the giant's hand.

Now colour in the butterfly.

The giant's castle

Can you add the windows to the castle walls?

Can you see Tom Thumb?

The Gingerbread Man

A little old man and a little old woman lived in a little cottage near a river. One day, the little old woman baked a Gingerbread Man. She rolled out the dough, cut out the body and used currants for eyes and chocolate drops for buttons.

When the little old woman opened the oven, out jumped the Gingerbread Man – he had come alive! The little old woman and the little old man chased after the Gingerbread Man. "Stop, stop!" they shouted, but the Gingerbread Man was too fast.

"Run, run as fast as you can! You can't catch me, I'm the Gingerbread Man!" he shouted.

At the end of the road was a hungry pig. He joined the chase! "Stop, stop!" they shouted, but the Gingerbread Man was too fast.

"Run, run as fast as you can! You can't catch me, I'm the Gingerbread Man!" he shouted.

They passed a hungry cow and she joined the chase! "Stop, stop!" they shouted, but the Gingerbread Man was too fast. "Run, run as fast as you can! You can't catch me, I'm the Gingerbread Man!" he shouted.

By the river was a hungry fox. He offered to help the Gingerbread Man across the river: "Jump on my tail and I'll swim you across." So the Gingerbread Man jumped on the fox's tail. But the fox was sly and instead of helping him across, he gobbled up the Gingerbread Man!

Gingerbread biscuit

Find the stickers to decorate the Gingerbread Man.

Match the men

Trace the lines and find the matching gingerbread men.

Thumbelina's giant flower

Colour in the petals of Thumbelina's flower.

How many petals can you count?

Pretty Thumbelina

Which Thumbelina is holding the red flowers?

And which Thumbelina is flying?

The prince needs help!

Help the prince find the correct path to his princess.

Treasure chest

Fill the treasure chest with stickers of golden objects.

Goldilocks and the Three Bears

A little girl with golden hair called Goldilocks went for a walk in the woods one day, and got very lost. She came across a cottage and knocked on the door. When there was no answer, Goldilocks went in.

Goldilocks was hungry. On the table were three steaming bowls of porridge. She tried the first bowl but it was too hot. The second bowl was too cold. The third bowl was just right so she ate it all up!

Goldilocks was tired. In the cottage there were three comfy chairs. She tried the first chair but it was too high. The second chair was too low. The third chair was just right but it broke when she sat in it!

Goldilocks was still tired. In the bedroom there were three beds. She tried the first bed but it was too hard. The second bed was too soft. The third bed was just right so she climbed in and fell fast asleep!

Then, the three bears who lived in the house came home, ready for their porridge.

"Who's been eating my porridge?" growled Daddy Bear. "Who's been eating my porridge?" asked Mummy Bear. "Somebody's been eating my porridge, and it's all gone!" cried Baby Bear!

"Who's been sitting in my chair?" growled Daddy Bear. "Who's been sitting in my chair?" asked Mummy Bear. "Somebody's been sitting in my chair, they've broken it!" cried Baby Bear!

"Who's been sleeping in my bed?" growled Daddy Bear. "Who's been sleeping in my bed?" asked Mummy Bear. "Somebody's been sleeping in my bed, and she's still there!" cried Baby Bear!

Goldilocks jumped up with a fright and ran out of the bedroom and out of the house.

The hungry bears

Can you lead the three bears to their porridge?

Find the bowls

Put the stickers of the three bowls of porridge on the table.

The Elves and the Shoemaker

Can you find the shoe stickers to fill the shelves?

Draw a shoe

Trace over the dotted line to draw the shoe.

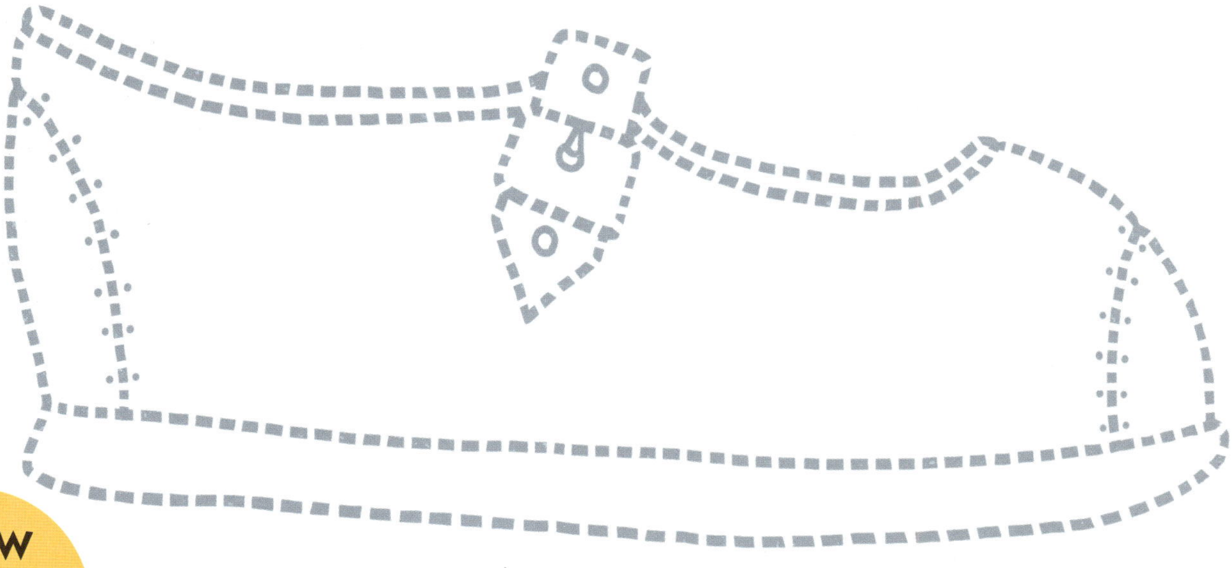

Now colour it in.

Pinocchio's long nose

Join the dots to complete Pinocchio's long nose!

1
5
2
3
4

Do you know what makes Pinocchio's nose grow long?

Counting Pinocchio's books

How many red books can you count?

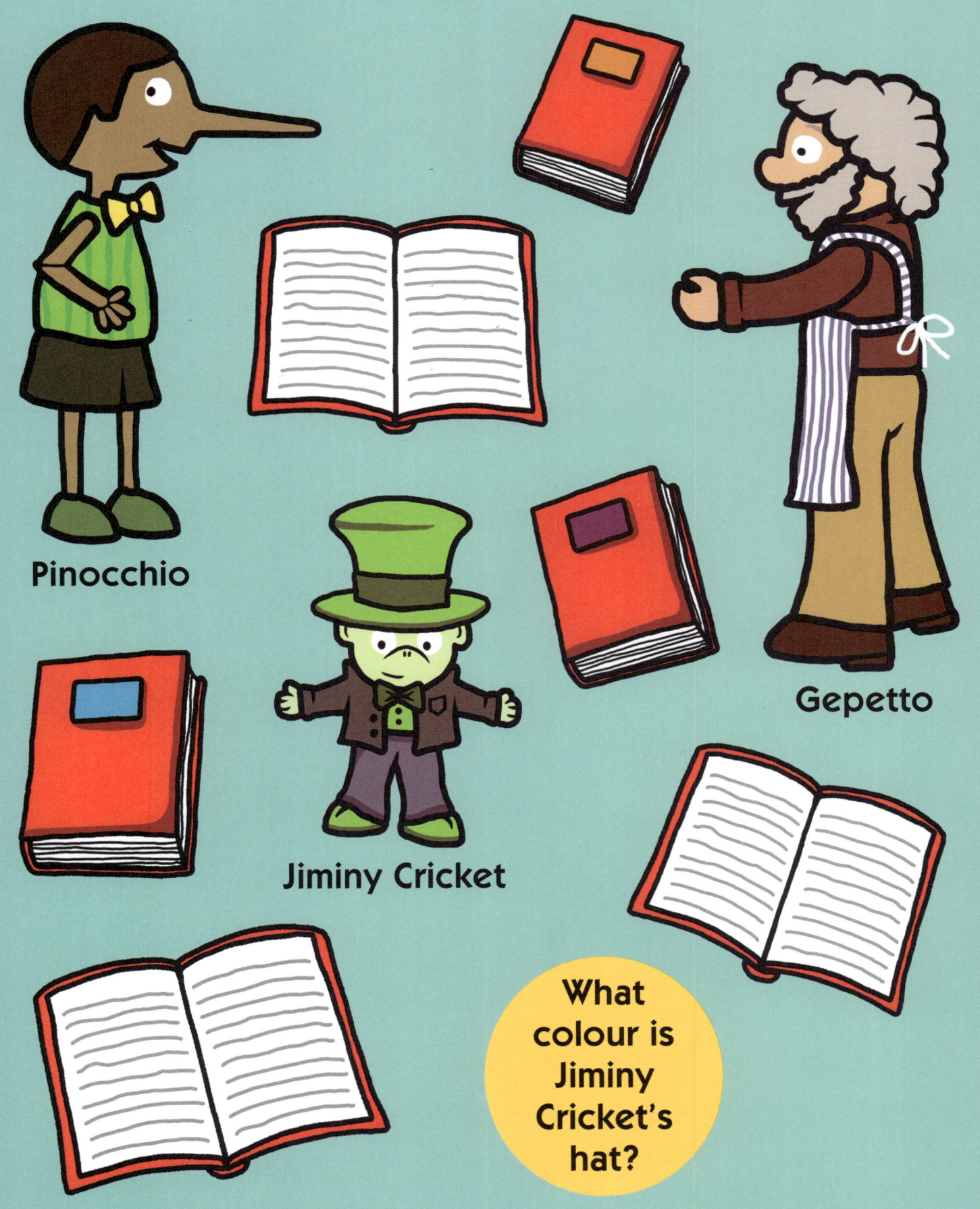

Pinocchio

Jiminy Cricket

Gepetto

What colour is Jiminy Cricket's hat?

The Princess and the Pea

Add some more mattress stickers to make the princess's bed.

Can you colour in the pea?